Just Keep Swimming

UNDERWATER VOLCANOES, TRENCHES AND RIDGES

GEOGRAPHY FOR KIDS

Patterns in the Physical Environment

www.ProfessorBeaver.ca

Published by Speedy Publishing Canada Limited

PROFESSOR
BEAVER
Building Smarter and Brighter Minds

CONTENTS

In this book, we're going to talk about underwater geography.

So, let's get right to it!

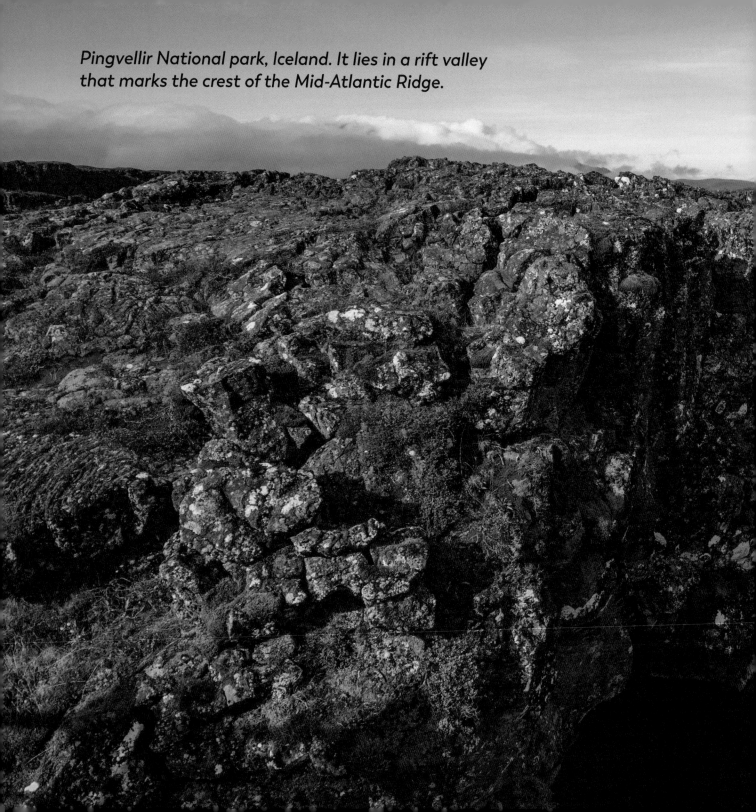

Þingvellir National park, Iceland. It lies in a rift valley that marks the crest of the Mid-Atlantic Ridge.

The bottoms of the oceans have different geographic structures just like the landforms on Earth's surface do. Some of the largest mountains and volcanoes on Earth are actually underwater!

For example, the longest range of mountains in the world is under the surface of the Atlantic Ocean. It's described as the Mid-Atlantic Ridge and its length is over 56,000 kilometers.

The Turtle Pits site on the mid-Atlantic Ridge, consisting of two sulfide mounds and a black smoker chimney. It is located 40,000 miles deep in the ridge

Oceanographers study the floor of the ocean and the words that they use to describe it are sometimes different than those used to describe the same feature on the surface of the land. For example, an underwater mountain is sometimes described as a seamount.

Here are some of the basic terms you should know in order to understand the geography at the bottom of the ocean floor.

- **TRENCH** - a long area of the ocean floor that is deeper than the surrounding area

- **TROUGH** - an area that slopes gently down compared to the surrounding area

◄ *A diver swims between the Eurasian and North American tectonic plates in Silfra Canyon, Thingvellir National Park, Iceland.*

- **ISLAND** - a landmass that is surrounded by water on all sides

- **RIDGE** - a part of the ocean floor that is a narrow strip of elevation

- **GAP** - a steep opening that goes through an underwater ridge of a mountain

- **SEAMOUNT** - a mountain that is underwater, rising at least 1,000 meters from the ocean floor

*A manta ray (Manta alfredi) swims over
a seamount in Raja Ampat, Indonesia*

the Ustyurt Plateau.

- **RISE** - a mountainous area formed by tectonic plates that are getting further apart

- **PLATEAU** - a large area that is at a higher elevation than the area around it and is almost flat.

- **VOLCANO** - fissures in the surface of the Earth that are underwater and erupt magma.

CROSS SECTION OF A VOLCANO

Cloud of volcanic ash
Volcanic bombs
Vent
Crater
Pipe
Cone
Lava flow
Ash layers
Magma
Magma chamber

A cross section. of an igneous volcano erupting.

16

- **HYDROTHERMAL VENT** - an opening in the floor of the ocean where water that is rich in minerals flows out.

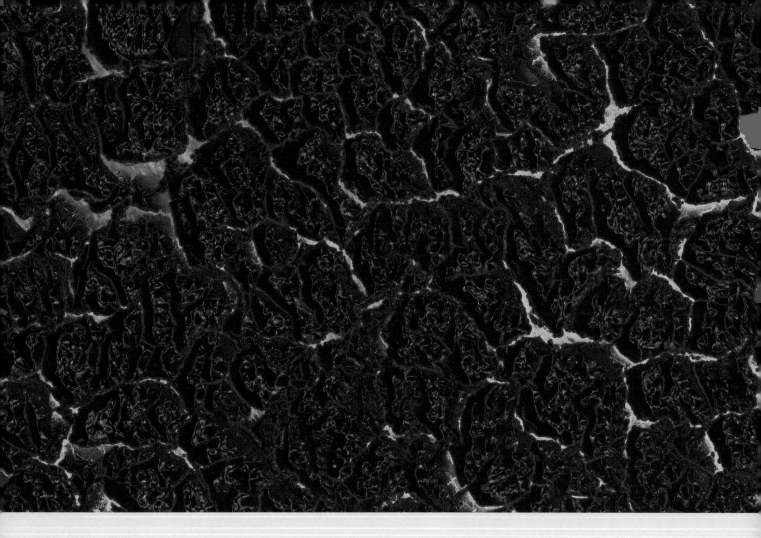

- **MAGMA** - hot, liquid rock that is under the surface of the Earth.

◄ *An image of a hydrothermal vent on the ocean floor*

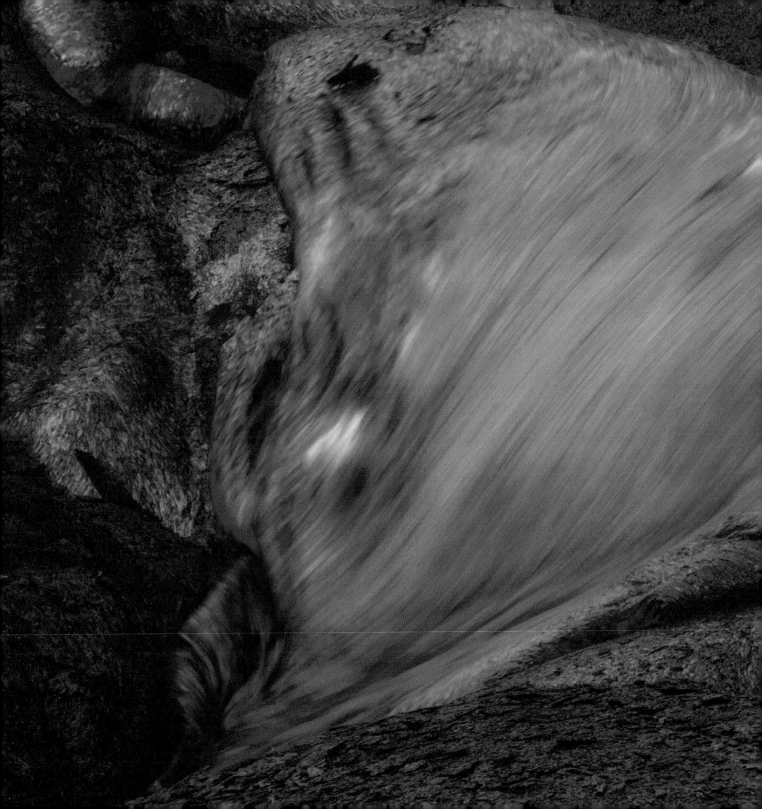

Lava Flow

20

- **LAVA** - hot, liquid rock that has erupted from a fissure or volcano, either on land or under water.

- **HYDROPHONE** - a high-tech microphone that can pick up sounds at a long distance under water.

Hydrophone being lowered into the Atlantic.

A hydrophone node

- **SUBDUCTION** - a collision of two tectonic plates where one moves over the other.

Underwater volcanoes

Crust

Rising mag

- **TSUNAMI** - a gigantic, destructive ocean wave caused by seismic activity.

UNDERWATER VOLCANOES

Oceanographers, who are scientists specializing in the study of the ocean, still have much to learn about the bottom of the ocean floor.

More than 75% of the magma that erupts from inside the Earth's core comes from volcanoes that are underwater. Most of these volcanoes are situated

near ridges in the ocean floor that have formed from the movement of tectonic plates.

Underwater volcanoes are usually located deep under the ocean's surface, but there are some that are close enough to the water's surface that they spew out material into the air.

At Brimstone Pit the pressure of 560 meters (1837 feet) of water over the site reduces the power of the explosive bursts.

It's common for hydrothermal vents to be found near these areas of volcanic activity. Scientists have found that many organisms thrive in the water from hydrothermal vents, even though the water is very hot.

White smoky vent fluid rises out of small sulfur chimneys at Northwest Eifuku volcano.

Most underwater volcanoes that are active produce a huge amount of lava rather than exploding eruptions. There are two reasons for this. In these volcanoes, the levels of gas, mostly carbon dioxide, from the magma are relatively low. Also, the pressure from the water that surrounds them prevents them from exploding often. However, it was proven recently that some underwater volcanoes do explode.

When volcanoes explode or erupt on land, it takes a while for the lava to cool.

◄ *White flocculent mats in and around the extremely gassy, high-temperature white smokers at Champagne Vent.*

However, because water is such a good conductor of heat, underwater lava often cools down much more quickly and is turned into a form of glass. There's another difference between underwater lava and lava that's on

Pillow lava at the Galapagos Rift.

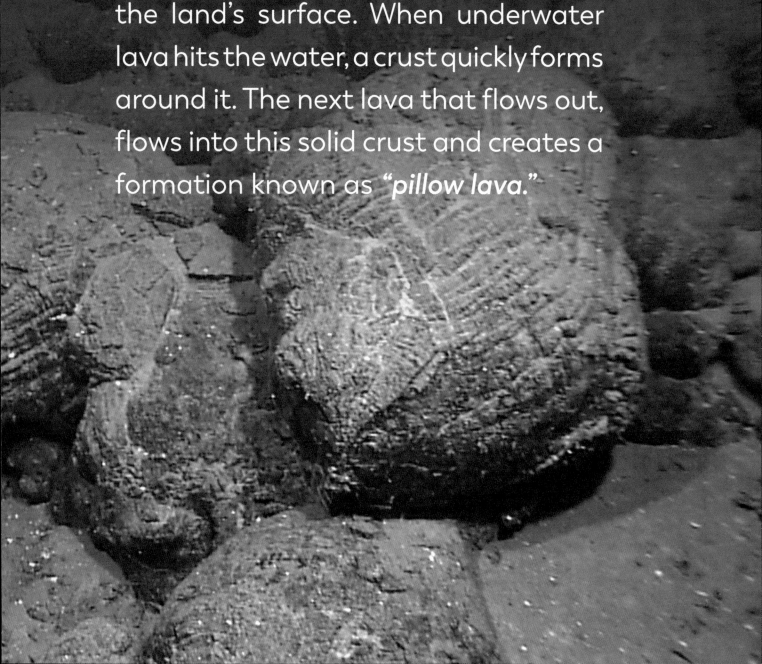

the land's surface. When underwater lava hits the water, a crust quickly forms around it. The next lava that flows out, flows into this solid crust and creates a formation known as *"pillow lava."*

34

It's estimated that there are at least 40,000 seamounts under the ocean. Some of these are underwater mountains or mountain ranges. Some are extinct volcanoes and some are active volcanoes.

Only a few seamounts have been studied in detail since many of them are at depths that are hundreds if not thousands of meters under the water's surface.

Orange glow of magma from West Mata submarine volcano. ▶

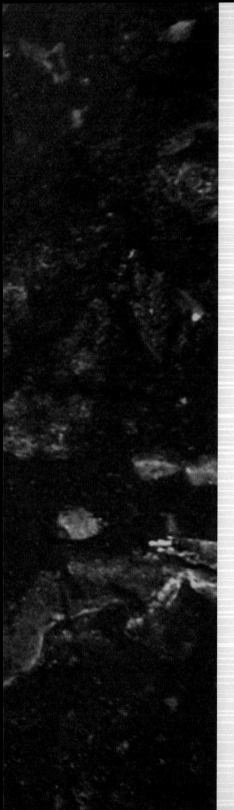

If an active volcano is more than 2,200 meters below the surface, it's harder to locate because water is under so much pressure at that depth that it doesn't boil. Without the boiling sounds that come from underwater volcanoes, it's difficult to locate them using hydrophones.

The orange glow of superheated magma. Pacific Ocean, Northeast Lau Basin, Fiji area.

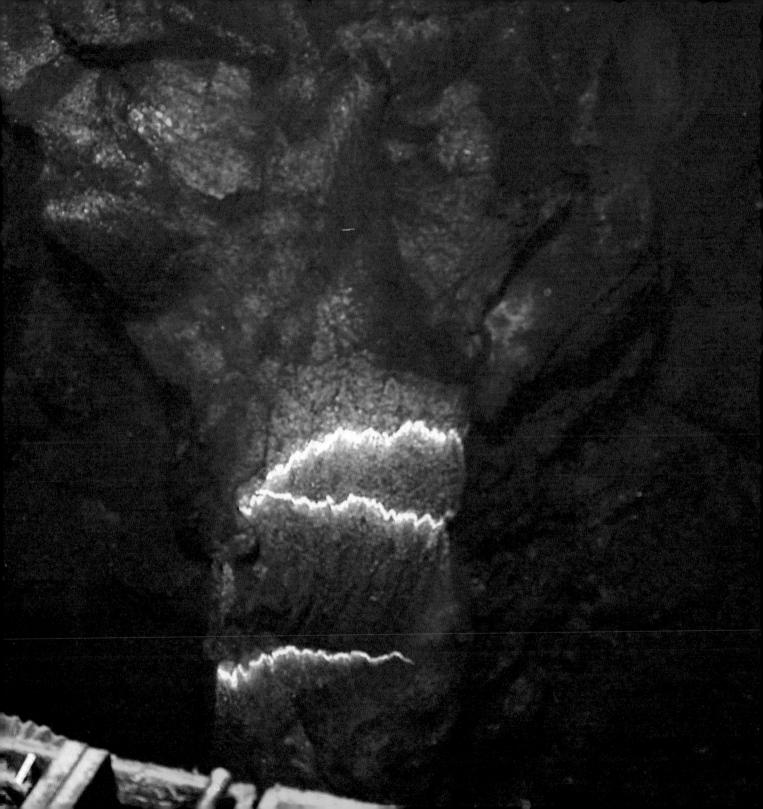

In 2009, scientists discovered one of the deepest volcanic eruptions ever found. The eruption was from the West Mata volcano, which is located 4,000 feet under the surface of the Pacific Ocean off the Tonga Ridge's north end.

It was emitting Boninite lavas, which are thought to be the hottest forms of lava to erupt on Earth. Scientists saw the lava traveling along the bottom of the ocean. They also witnessed deep-sea shrimp swimming nearby in the very hot water.

◄ *Bands of glowing magma, about 2,200 degrees Fahrenheit, are exposed as a pillow lava tube extrudes down slope.*

40

The largest underwater volcano in the world is thought to be Tamu Massif, which is about 1,000 miles off the eastern coast of Japan. This enormous shield volcano has a dome that is more than 100,000 square miles, about the size of the entire state of New Mexico!

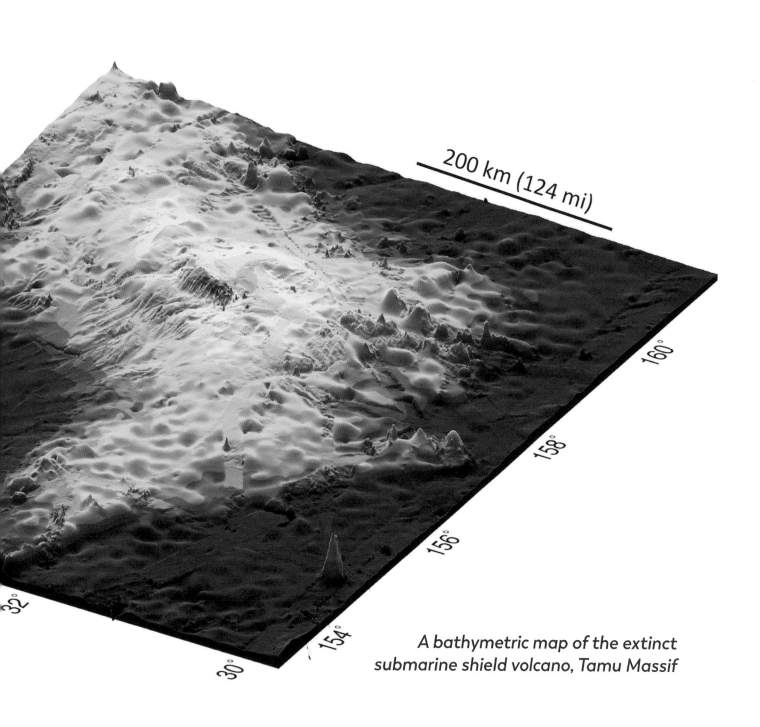

200 km (124 mi)

160°

158°

156°

32°

30°

154°

A bathymetric map of the extinct submarine shield volcano, Tamu Massif

Section of the Earth's crust.

It's one of the biggest volcanoes in the entire solar system. At the beginning, scientists believed that it was made up of several smaller volcanoes, but recent research points to the fact that it is one massive volcano. It's a good thing that this volcano isn't active. It hasn't erupted for about 145 million years.

TRENCHES

The deepest of all the ocean trenches on Earth is the Mariana Trench in the Pacific Ocean. It was created by the Pacific and Philippine tectonic plates. As the larger Pacific plate slides over the smaller Philippine plate, the smaller plate goes down into the Earth's mantle.

This process, which is called subduction, forms the deep shape of the trench. The

Mariana Trench is located just south of the country of Japan and east of the Philippines. The deepest region of the trench is called the Challenger Deep. It is a whopping 35,797 feet below the sea's surface.

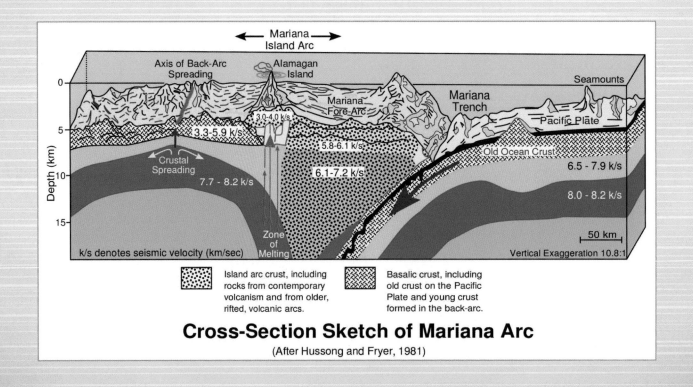

Cross-Section Sketch of Mariana Arc

(After Hussong and Fryer, 1981)

Only a few people have been down that far because the water pressure is immense and it requires traveling in special equipment, such as high-tech submarines and bathyscaphes.

In 2012, Hollywood director James Cameron went down to the bottom of the Challenger Deep. The trench is more than 100 times larger than the size of the Grand Canyon and it is deeper than the height of the tallest mountain on Earth, Mount Everest.

A school of fish swimming around active volcanic vents that are emitting sulphurous gases and that lies close to an active subduction zone.

50

The Tonga Trench extends from the North Island of New Zealand in a northeast direction to Tonga. It's a distance of more than 1,500 miles. The Tonga Trench was created by the Pacific and Tonga tectonic plates.

It contains the Horizon Deep, which is located at a depth of 35,702 feet below the sea's surface. The movement of plates there has caused massive volcanoes to disappear into the Earth.

Amphipoda - inhabitant of the Kara Sea ▶

In 2013, researchers from Japan went down into Horizon Deep and they brought back a specimen of a prawn-like creature called an amphipod. It lives as deep as 20,000 feet below sea level.

52

It has no pigment and it lives in total darkness under an enormous amount of water pressure. Oceanographers and other scientists are finding sea creatures at depths that they never thought were possible.

Plate subductioin

The deepest trench in the Atlantic Ocean is the Puerto Rico Trench. It is located due north of Puerto Rico and is formed by the North American tectonic plate and the Caribbean tectonic plate. The trench is 28,232 feet in depth.

The collision of the two plates causes earthquakes just as other plate collisions do worldwide. The movements of the plates can also cause very destructive tsunamis.

RIDGES

Imagine the seams that stand up on the surface of a baseball. This is similar to how the mid-ocean ridge looks on a map. The mid-ocean ridge is a series of volcanoes that connect with each other under the oceans. If you saw a map of them, they would seem like wavy lines running down the middle of the oceans.

56

This system is actually a continuous seam that travels around the Earth for more than 40,000 miles. The interconnecting ridges are formed by places where tectonic plates are moving away from each other and new flows of molten rock are pushing up to the ocean floor from the Earth's mantle.

Thingvellir national park Iceland - North American - Europe lithospheric rift - Mid-Atlantic Ridge

59

SUMMARY

The geography of the surface of the ocean floor is filled with volcanoes, both extinct and active, and underwater mountains. In fact, there is more volcanic activity under the ocean than there is on the Earth's surface.

In addition to active volcanoes and extensive underwater mountain ranges, there are very deep trenches, some over 6 miles deep, and narrow strips of elevation called ridges. The deeper you go down, the more intense the water pressure gets.

Scientists have been surprised to discover sea creatures that live in depths of water not thought possible before.

Awesome! Now that you've read about underwater geography, you may want to read about what happens when volcanoes erupt in the Baby Professor book Kaboom! What Happens When Volcanoes Erupt? Geology for Beginners | Children's Geology Books.

Visit

 PROFESSOR
BEAVER
Building Smarter and Brighter Minds

www.ProfessorBeaver.ca

to download Free Professor Beaver eBooks
and view our catalog of new and exciting
Children's Books

Printed in Great Britain
by Amazon